ARCHITECTURE TOURS L.A. GUIDEBOOK
HOLLYWOOD

Architecture Tours L.A. Guidebook
HOLLYWOOD

Laura Massino Smith

Schiffer Publishing Ltd®
4880 Lower Valley Road, Atglen, PA 19310 USA

Library of Congress Cataloging-in-Publication Data

Smith, Laura Massino.
Architecture tours L.A. guidebook : Hollywood / by Laura Massino Smith.
p. cm.
ISBN 0-7643-2121-8 (pbk.)
1. Architecture—California—Los Angeles—Tours. 2. Automobile travel—California—Los Angeles—Tours. 3. Los Angeles (Calif.)—Buildings, structures, etc.—Tours. 4. Hollywood (Los Angeles, Calif.)—Buildings, structures, etc.—Tours. I. Title: Hollywood. II. Title.
NA735.L55S552 2004
720'.9794'94—dc22
2004014290

Designed by John P. Cheek
Type set in Futura BdCn BT/Humanist 521 LT BT
ISBN: 0-7643-2121-8
Printed in China
1 2 3 4

Dedication

To my extraordinary husband, Drew, whose undying love, patience, encouragement, and support have guided me to discover my true passion.

Published by Schiffer Publishing Ltd.
4880 Lower Valley Road
Atglen, PA 19310
Phone: (610) 593-1777; Fax: (610) 593-2002
E-mail: Info@schifferbooks.com

For the largest selection of fine reference books on this and related subjects, please visit our web site at **www.schifferbooks.com**
We are always looking for people to write books on new and related subjects. If you have an idea for a book please contact us at the above address.

This book may be purchased from the publisher.
Include $3.95 for shipping.
Please try your bookstore first.
You may write for a free catalog.

In Europe, Schiffer books are distributed by
Bushwood Books
6 Marksbury Ave.
Kew Gardens
Surrey TW9 4JF England
Phone: 44 (0) 20 8392-8585; Fax: 44 (0) 20 8392-9876
E-mail: info@bushwoodbooks.co.uk
Free postage in the U.K., Europe; air mail at cost.

ARCHITECTURE TOURS L.A.

www.architecturetoursla.com
323.464.7868

Architecture Tours L.A. specializes in guided driving tours led by an architectural historian in a 1962 vintage Cadillac. Our tours focus on the historic and significant contemporary architecture in Los Angeles, highlighting the cultural aspects of the history of the city's built environment. This guidebook will allow you to drive yourself and discover L.A. in your own car, at your own pace. In addition to HOLLYWOOD, other tours offered by Architecture Tours L.A. include:

DOWNTOWN
HANCOCK PARK/MIRACLE MILE
WEST HOLLYWOOD/BEVERLY HILLS
SILVER LAKE
PASADENA
FRANK GEHRY

Disclaimer

It is not advisable for anyone operating a motor vehicle to read this book. Please pull your car into a safe, designated parking area before attempting any fine print. Better yet, take this tour with a friend who can act as navigator and narrator. Naturally, the best way to see it all is riding shotgun with the author!

Neither the author nor the publisher assume responsibility for moving violations committed while intoxicated by this tour.

NOTE TO TOUR GOERS

The sites included in this self-guided tour represent the architectural highlights of the HOLLYWOOD area. This tour is meant to be an overview, a starting point of sorts, and is intended to give the participant a feeling for the neighborhood. By no means does the tour include everything of interest. Numerous books of ponderous proportions have been written to that end, and if your interest is piqued, you might refer to the bibliography in the back of this book for further reading.

Herein, within a matter of hours you will glean a pretty good understanding of what historically happened, and what is currently happening architecturally in HOLLYWOOD. The photographs herein are for quick identification of what you will be seeing up close, in full scale.

The criteria for inclusion into this guidebook consist of the historical, cultural, and architectural significance of each site, and the fact that it can be seen relatively easily from the street. So relax and have a great ride!

Introduction

Hollywood...probably the most famous city and most popular tourist destination in all of the world! Home to the Hollywood Walk of Fame, movie studios, movie stars, and so much great architecture – believe it or not!

Hollywood began very humbly with agriculture and small-town values. Acres and acres of orange groves dominated the town's crop production, but avocados, other citrus fruits, and horse ranches were here, too. In the late 1880s, however, all that began to change. Horace and Daeida Wilcox, a devout Methodist couple, came here from Kansas hoping to develop Hollywood into a calm, peaceful, bucolic haven far from rowdy Downtown Los Angeles, which at that time was a "Wild West" town. Some say they named Hollywood after a friend's country home back in Kansas, while others say it was because the Holy Wood of the Cross was here – a place blessed by Father Junipero Serra as he came through during the Spanish Expeditions, a trip which led to the establishment of the California Missions. The Wilcoxes purchased over 100 acres of land and began to develop it. They gave a parcel of land for free to anyone who wanted to build a church. They also managed to secede from the city of Los Angeles, becoming the City of Hollywood, where alcohol, movie theaters, and slaughterhouses were all banned. That only lasted a few years, however, and by 1910 Hollywood was a part of Los Angeles again, as it has been ever since. Residential and commercial development slowly emerged in this area and there were once large homes belonging to the prominent families of Hollywood along Hollywood Boulevard, but all have been demolished except the Janes family home.

The economic boom of the 1920s and the increasing growth of the movie industry fueled Hollywood's growth, and that period gave rise to some of the most significant architecture in the area. During this time the Art Deco style dominated as a way to show the sophistication of a growing city. The Spanish Colonial Revival style, which was also very popular, was a reminder of the city's history. Neo-Classical and Beaux-Arts styles were used for banks and other institutional-type buildings to create a sense of stability. The French Chateauesque style also proliferated in the 1920s due to the nation's exposure to France during World War I, after which people brought back what they had seen there. The fantasy of the film industry encouraged the creation of the "Storybook" style, which mimicked English cottages or Normandy farmhouses and created an instant sense of history. Also, the exotic architectural styles of Egypt and China were well suited to the design of theaters, representing faraway lands and providing even more escapism offered to audiences by the movies shown there.

Many cultural luminaries and actors were residents of Hollywood. Writers including Aldous Huxley, Charles Bukowski, and Raymond Chandler all lived here at one time or another. Will and Ariel Durant, who wrote the *History of Civilization*, lived in the Hollywood Hills. Nathaniel West, author of *Day of the Locusts*, Bertolt Brecht, the German poet, playwright, and theater director, and photographic artist Man Ray also lived here. Arts and culture flourished throughout Los Angeles.

Hollywood, especially Hollywood Boulevard, has been through many dramatic changes. In the 1950s and 1960s, much of the ornamentation of the Art Deco and Spanish Colonial Revival styles was lost. Many of the details were just covered over with signage or other covering. After World War II, Americans didn't want to look back at their history, and the focus became firmly fixed on the future. Hollywood Boulevard became a dark and dangerous place in the 1960s and 1970s. Nightly street activity consisted of drug deals, prostitution, and all that comes with that. Tourists didn't want to come to Hollywood for fear of the crime, and locals went to other areas of the city for their entertainment.

Fortunately, all that began to change in the 1980s. Hollywood, very slowly at first, began to get back its shine. Due to the restoration efforts of the city of Los Angeles and many private individuals, Hollywood started to regain what it had lost. The restoration of the Egyptian Theater was one of the first to see new life as the showcase for the American Cinematheque. Years later the Pig 'N Whistle restaurant was completely restored to its 1927 glamour, and many others followed, turning Hollywood around and bringing back a thriving entertainment and retail life to Hollywood Boulevard. Now there are many restored theaters, restaurants, and nightclubs, as well as new constructions – such as the Sunset-Vine Complex which combines the restoration of a historic structure with new construction, and a new retail center at Hollywood and Highland. There's even a new Greyhound bus station, bringing bus travel into the modern age. On this tour, you will see a mixture of Old Hollywood and New Hollywood as you enjoy the beautiful architecture of one great big tourist attraction!

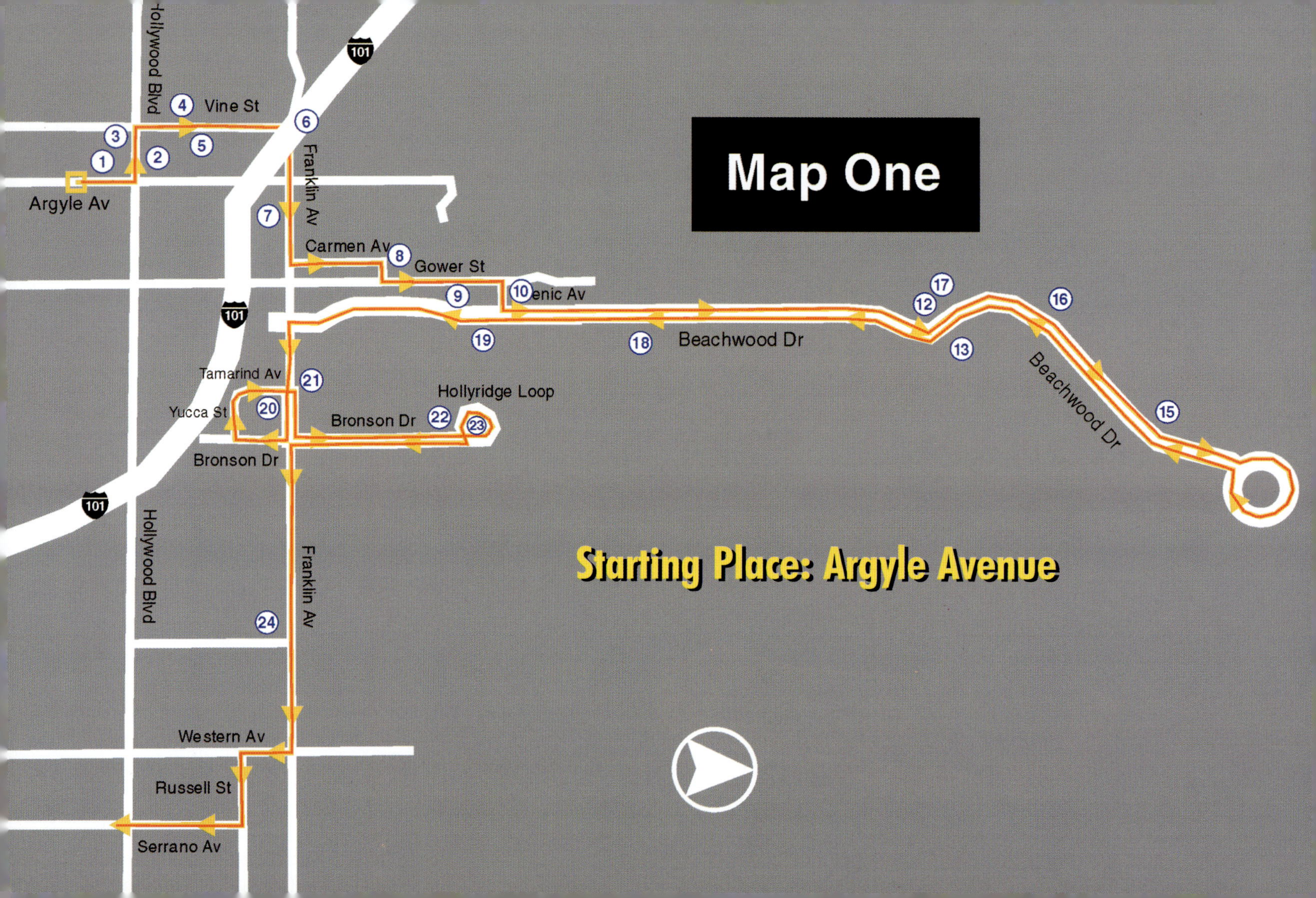

Map One
Starting Place: Argyle Avenue
Argyle Av
Hollywood Blvd
Vine St
Franklin Av
Carmen Av
Gower St
Beachwood Dr
Tamarind Av
Yucca St
Bronson Dr
Hollyridge Loop
Western Av
Russell St
Serrano Av
101

On Argyle Avenue: One block east of Vine Street just south of Hollywood Blvd.

1) On the corner of Argyle Avenue and Hollywood Blvd. is the Hollywood and Vine Metro subway station, completed in 1999. The theme of the station is "Hollywood" and on the street surface, icons of Hollywood are represented. Most obvious is the green, yellow, blue, and red pagoda-shaped structure made to represent the famous Chinese Theater further down on Hollywood Blvd. On the far corner is a brown, hat-shaped shelter, which is a reminder that the famous Brown Derby restaurant was once nearby. There were originally four Brown Derby restaurants, all alluding to the derby hat shape. They were owned by the second husband of screen star Gloria Swanson and were a celebrity hangout. All are gone now, but the shelter is reminiscent of what was once here. The elevator that leads down to the station itself is enclosed in glass block and has a movie marquee above, which symbolizes the movie industry in Hollywood. The shelter in the shape of a white stretch limousine symbolizes the "glamour" of Hollywood. Down below the street surface are more icons of Hollywood in the form of faux palm trees, antique movie cameras, and empty metal film reels that line the ceiling. Images of Hollywood drawn by local children have been made into wall tiles and incorporated into the design scheme.

1) Hollywood/Vine Metro Subway Station, 1999, corner of Hollywood Blvd. and Argyle Avenue

From this station you can travel all the way to Downtown Los Angeles where connections with other trains can be made. This line goes as far north as North Hollywood, just into the San Fernando Valley, and as far west as Hollywood and Highland right next to the Chinese Theater. The Gold Line, opened in 2003, is the newest line, and from Downtown it goes northeast to Pasadena and Sierra Madre. The Metro line also goes as far south as Long Beach, and if you switch trains twice from here you can get all the way to LAX airport.

Plans are currently underway for a high-rise development at this site.

Continue north on Argyle Avenue

2) Here on the northwest corner of Argyle Avenue and Hollywood Blvd. is the Pantages Theater, built in 1929. This was the last of three Pantages Theaters to be built in L.A. for Alexander Pantages (the other two are located in Downtown). This theater was designed by the same architect as the others in the exuberant Art Deco style. The visual characteristics include the use of stylized floral forms, flattened V-shaped chevron patterns, and full-size idealized heroic figures. The rich detailing of the lobby includes black marble and gold leaf, and is carried out on the interior, which was designed by Anthony Heinsbergen, designer of a number of theater interiors throughout the city. This was thought to be one of the most glamorous theaters, and many of the Academy Award presentations were held here. Badly damaged in the 1994 6.8 Northridge Earthquake, it was completely restored and reopened with Disney's production of *The Lion King* in 1999. This location is listed as Historic-Cultuı al Monument #193 by the City of Los Angeles and is included in the Hollywood Boulevard Commercial and Entertainment District.

2) The Pantages Theater Building, 1929, B. Marcus Priteca, 6233 Hollywood Blvd.

In the early 1980s the Hollywood Boulevard Commercial and Entertainment District was designated by the National Trust for Historic Preservation. The area between Hollywood Blvd. at Argyle Avenue and continuing west to Highland Avenue, with some branches on Vine Street, Ivar Avenue, and others, represents an excellent sampling of the architectural styles prevalent during approximately 1915-1935 when there was great prosperity and growth, mostly due to the film industry.

Turn left onto Hollywood Blvd. Turn right on Vine Street

3) The idea for one of the world's greatest tourist attractions belongs to the Hollywood Chamber of Commerce – images of five-pointed stars embedded into the terrazzo sidewalk with the names of Hollywood stars and the branches of the entertainment industry for which they are honored. There are four categories a performer can be nominated for, including motion pictures, television, radio and recording, and live theater. A committee decides whether or not to designate a star for that person, and then a ceremony is held with the performer, fan club members, people on the street, and Chamber of Commerce officials. Thus history is made. Approximately fifteen to twenty new stars are added every year. This location is listed as Historic-Cultural Monument #194 by the City of Los Angeles.

3)Hollywood Walk of Fame, 1961, Hollywood Chamber of Commerce, Hollywood Blvd. and Vine Street

4) Here on your left, originally a theater for Vaudeville in the 1920s, it was also the broadcast location of television's *The Lawrence Welk Show* and *This Is Your Life* in the 1950s and 1960s. Currently the home of a fashionable nightclub, the theater was designed in the flamboyant Spanish Colonial Revival style. This style, as well as the Art Deco style, was very popular in the 1920s. It is characterized by very ornate surface decoration in the form of scrolls and foliage, devil's heads, shield shapes (with the initials "HPH" for Hollywood Play House), fountains, and a crown at the top. All meant to depict a feeling of strength, power, and history, alluding to the historical reference of Spain's colonization of Mexico and California. This location is included in the Hollywood Boulevard Commercial and Entertainment District.

4) Hollywood Play House (now Avalon nightclub), 1927, Gogerty and Weyl, 1735 Vine Street

5) **Capitol Records Tower Building, 1954, Welton Becket and Associates (Louis Naidorf), 1750 Vine Street**

Continue up the hill Turn right on Franklin Avenue

6) Just beyond the crest of the hill you will be passing under the Hollywood Freeway, also know as the 101 Freeway, which was built in 1954.

6) Hollywood Freeway, 1954

7) The Hollywood Tower apartment building, on your right, was built in the late 1920s in the Chateauesque style, another popular style of the era. The interior of the building is in the Art Deco style, as is the neon sign outside. The apartments are spacious, however, close to the Freeway. The Hollywood Tower is listed on the National Register of Historic Places.

7) The Hollywood Tower (a.k.a. La Belle Tour), 1929, Cramer & Wise, 6200 Franklin Avenue

Turn left on Carmen Ave.

8) At the end of this quiet residential street is of all things, a monastery. Right in the middle of Hollywood is the Monastery of the Angels, where a cloistered order of Dominican nuns live and work. There were larger numbers when the monastery opened in the late 1940s, but now more than twenty nuns are still here, praying and making Monastery bread and chocolates. The gift shop and chapel are open to the public. Well-known Los Angeles architect Wallace Neff designed the building in the Spanish Mediterranean style as a peaceful retreat in the foothills of Hollywood. Their patron saint is St. Michael, the archangel, whose likeness can be seen in the statue near the entrance. Some have noted that the statue bears resemblance to the Academy Awards Oscar statuette.

8) Monastery of the Angels, Chapel of the Perpetual Adoration, 1947, Wallace Neff, 1977 Carmen Place

Turn left on Gower Street

9) Here on the right is a white stucco house composed of a juxtaposition of forms. A flared side wall, an arched front entrance, and glass door intersect with a sharp 90-degree angle to create a striking dynamic. The palette of the Dutch artist Piet Mondrian is used on the garage and front doors to contrast against the white stucco.

9) Rajogopal House, 1983, Paul Sterling Hoag, 2122 Gower Street

Turn right on Scenic Avenue

10) Here on your left is a pristine example of the French Chateauesque style popular in the 1920s and 1930s. Complete with turrets with conical spires and a steeply pitched roof, it is a replica of a French Chateau, originally designed as apartments and converted to condominiums in 1989. The popularity of this style has to do with the fact that as a nation we had been to France during World War I, after which the style traveled back to this country. It also exemplifies the "fantasy" lifestyle, and feeling as though one lives in a castle. This was once home to Marilyn Monroe and Madonna.

10) Chateau Beachwood, 1937, Walter C. King, 6501-6061 Scenic Avenue and 2203-2205 Beachwood Drive

Turn left on Beachwood Drive

11) Directly in front of you and perched on Mount Lee is the famous Hollywood Sign. It was erected in 1923 to advertise a 500-acre subdivision of real estate that the Hollywoodland Realty Company was trying to sell. Originally, it spelled out H-O-L-L-Y-W-O-O-D-L-A-N-D, but the word LAND was removed in 1945 when the sign was donated to the city. Years earlier, in 1932, rising starlet Peg Entwistle, feeling desperate from a struggling film career, jumped off the top of the letters and was gone forever. The legend says that the very next day she had a phone call from someone offering her a part in a movie! The Hollywood sign was made of wood and the letters were outlined in light bulbs. By 1978 the sign had deteriorated and a new sign was constructed with funds donated by various celebrities. At $27,700.00 a letter, Gene Autry purchased an "L," Hugh Hefner threw a fund-raising party for the "H," and rock musician Alice Cooper bought the last "O" in honor of Graucho Marx. For the millennium celebration on December 31st, 1999, a fireworks spectacular was planned; however, due to rain that day, it was canceled and a lackluster lightshow was displayed for all of fifteen minutes. The sign is no longer lit. This location is listed as Historic-Cultural Monument #111 by the City of Los Angeles.

11) Hollywood Sign, 1923, Mount Lee

12) You should now be approaching the grey sandstone gates to Hollywoodland. The gates were also constructed in 1923 as part of the development to let you know that you were entering an exclusive neighborhood. Notice the faux chimney and the clock on the back side, which usually keeps the correct time. This location is listed as Historic-Cultural Monument #20 by the City of Los Angeles.

12) Hollywoodland Gates, 1923, European craftsmen, Beachwood Drive

13) This is the original office for Hollywoodland Realty and is still operating as a real estate office. It is in the style of many of the houses in the neighborhood, now known as "Storybook." It is a mixture of English Tudor, French, and Bavarian architectural styles.

13) Hollywoodland Realty Company, 1923, John De Lario, 2700 North Beachwood Drive

Bear to the left
Continue up the hill on Beachwood Drive

14) The dominant styles of architecture in 1920s Hollywoodland were Spanish Mediterranean, English Tudor, Storybook, and French Provincial. Currently, nearly every conceivable architectural style co-exits with the original homes – from Craftsman to Modern and Post-modern, as well as those hybrid styles more difficult to categorize.

With meandering mountain roads, lush greenery, quiet, and privacy, the Hollywood hills are the most desirable part of Hollywood. Many of the homes are now comfortably nestled into the landscaping, and to many residents it is like living in the country, while the bustling city is only a few minutes away. That country feeling is enhanced by the presence of coyotes, skunks, and deer, as well as other wild animals that also like living in the hills. At one time or another Humphrey Bogart, Bela Lugosi, Doris Day, Ned Beatty, and Darryl Hannah have all lived in Hollywoodland.

14) Various Houses in Hollywoodland, c. 1920s, Beachwood Drive

Go all the way to the end of the street where you will see one of the entrances to Griffith Park and the Sunset Ranch (where you can rent horses and ride through the hills).
Make a U-turn
Go back down the hill.

15) On the right, built into the hillside where the road ascends the hill is a relatively new addition to Hollywoodland. Just 1700 square feet inside and barely 15 feet wide, the house appears as a massive concrete box. It is composed of a steel and wood integrated frame. Large windows and twenty-foot high ceilings make the most of the interior space. Designed by husband/wife team, Sarah Graham and Marc Angelil, both of whom teach architecture, this house also houses their studio above the garage, which has a separate entrance from the house. Concrete blocks and walls allude to the Brutalist style of architecture from the 1950s-1970s and provide a sharp contrast to the lush greenery all around. The overhanging, tilted flat roof looks like a lid topping a box.

15) "Experimental House," 1996, Angelil/Graham, 6009 Rodgerton Drive

16) On the right are the Hollywoodland Steps, built of granite stone in 1923 as part of the original development to be a short-cut to the street above. One hundred forty-eight very steep steps take you to Belden Drive above. Originally, there were planters and a beautiful trickling stream of water running down the middle. For years the planters were dormant, having been covered over with cement, but in 2002, the planters were restored, and maybe one day the water will run again. This location is listed as Historic-Cultural Monument #535 by the City of Los Angeles.

17) Directly in front of you is the Beachwood Market. The section with the tall glass wall is the 1954 expansion designed by important modern architect John Lautner. A curved ceiling with recessed lighting can be seen inside, giving a space-age update to the Spanish Mediterranean market.

16) Hollywoodland Steps, 1923, Woodshire Drive

17) Beachwood Market Expansion, 1954, John Lautner, 2699 Beachwood Drive

Go back through the gates Continue down Beachwood Drive

18) Here on your left, just past Cheremoya Avenue, the apartment building with the address of the building and the stars gracing the surface is an example of a "dingbat." Dingbats were known as the ornamentation for these rather simple stucco box apartment buildings that went up in the 1950s and 1960s. Now dingbat refers to the type of building seen all over Los Angeles. It was a way of dressing-up these inexpensive dwellings. Often the building was elevated and the parking would be at street level underneath the apartments.

18) "Dingbat" Apartments, c. 1957, (architect unknown), 2488 Beachwood Drive

19) Hollywood is a very transient place, so there are many apartment buildings of all styles. One of the most remarkable apartment buildings on this street is here on your left, past Beachwood Terrace. The "Venita Beachwood" is a rare example of exuberance of expression and gracious apartment living. The contractor was Charles Strolsee, but the only name listed as architect on the original building permit from 1925 was "Martin." There is no way of telling whether this was a first or last name, but the important names associated with this building are Chaplin and Sennett. Silent screen actor Charlie Chaplin and silent screen filmmaker Mack Sennett, who worked with Chaplin and whose "Keystone Company" made the Keystone Cops silent comedies, were partners in the investment of the Venita Beachwood. Originally built as a residential hotel, it is a replica of an Italian Venetian residence and is complete with rows of arched windows, twisted columns in front, and barber-pole striped fence posts tilted on an angle as they would be in the waters of Venice, Italy.

19) "Venita Beachwood" Apartments, 1925, (? *Martin*), 2028 Beachwood Drive

Turn left on Franklin Avenue
Right on Bronson Avenue
Right on Yucca Street
Continue around to Tamarind

20) The soaring, massive French Chateauesque style building is the original Chateau Elysee, another residential hotel built in the late 1920s by architect Arthur E. Harvey for the Ince Development Company. It was commissioned by Eleanor Ince, wife of Thomas Ince, the silent screen filmmaker and studio owner whose death, which occurred on the yacht of William Randolph Hearst, is shrouded in mystery. It is rumored that after Ince's death Hearst invested in the hotel. Humphrey Bogart, Clark Gable, Carole Lombard, and Ginger Rogers were guests here, as was Elizabeth Taylor, and more recently, Tom Cruise. In the 1950s, the hotel was transformed into a retirement home for actors and in 1972 it was acquired by the Church of Scientology. It was then restored and is now a retreat hotel for Scientology members. The restaurant is open to the public. This location is listed as Historic-Cultural Monument #329 by the City of Los Angeles.

20) The Manor Hotel, formerly the Chateau Elysee (now Church of Scientology Celebrity Centre), 1927-1929, Arthur E. Harvey, 5930 Franklin Avenue

Stop at the corner of Tamarind Avenue and Franklin Avenue

21) Villa Carlotta Apartments, 1926, Arthur E. Harvey, 5959 Franklin Avenue

21) Directly across from you are the Villa Carlotta Apartments, designed by the same architect and a year earlier than the Chateau Elysee. It is in the Spanish Mediterranean style as characterized by the arches, columns, and terra cotta roof. This was said to at one time have been the staff quarters for the employees of the Chateau Elysee and that there was a tunnel connecting the two buildings that workers used to get from one building to the next. The original estimate for construction was $200,000 for the one hundred fourteen room apartment building. In 1930, Louella Parsons, the famed Hollywood gossip columnist, was married here and kept an apartment and office here for many years. This location is listed as Historic-Cultural Monument #315 by the City of Los Angeles.

Right on Franklin Avenue Left on Bronson Avenue

22) Here on your left is the house affectionately known as the "Gingerbread House." Built by Mr. Kahn of the Kahn Construction Company, it is a fine example of the English Tudor style. Mixing brick and half-timber (half wood/half masonry) construction materials and methods, it has settled into its landscaping comfortably.

22) S.H. Kahn ("Gingerbread") House, 1923, Kahn Construction Company, 2127 North Bronson

Turn left onto Hollyridge Loop

23) On the island in the center of Hollyridge Loop is a house built the same year as the one just seen. This house combines characteristics of various styles. The arched colonnade in front is of the Mission style, the front door with its pointed arch is reminiscent of the Gothic style, the horseshoe and diamond shaped windows are Moorish, and the terra cotta roof is Mediterranean. Put all together it works as a whole. From the 1960s to the 1980s the house was owned by musician Chuck Berry, and then broken up into apartments and rented out. In 2001 it was sold to investors, who have restored the house to its former glory.

23) E.I. McCray House, 1923, Edward E. Sweet, 2151 Hollyridge Loop

Continue around the loop
Go back down Bronson Avenue
Turn left on Franklin Avenue

24) Since the late 1980s there have been numerous restoration projects underway in Hollywood; so much so that people have said that Hollywood is experiencing a "Renaissance." Some of the projects have been quite involved and others have been, more or less, cosmetic in scope. The Franklin Plaza Apartments, here on the right, were in terrible condition for many years, with overgrown trees hiding the dingy grey building. In the mid-1990s, the building, designed by the same architects who designed the Hollywood Tower seen earlier, was revived. It was painted with a polychromatic scheme, which highlighted the architectural details, and the overgrown foliage was cut back so the building could finally be seen. The style combines elements of Spanish Mediterranean, Italian Renaissance Revival, and Neo-Classical architecture.

24) The Franklin Plaza Apartments, 1928, Cramer & Wise, 5640 Franklin Avenue

Turn right on Western Avenue
Left on Russell Street
Right on Serrano

Map Two

Serrano Av
Loma Linda Av
Harvard Dr
Franklin Av
Franklin Av
Vermont Av
Los Feliz Blvd
Cromwell Av
Glendower Av
Glendower Av
Observatory
Hollywood Blvd
Lyman Pl
Clayton Av
Hillhurst Av
Hillhurst Av
Los Feliz Blvd
25
26
27
28
29
30
31
32
33
34
35
36

25) The Trianon Apartments, 1928, Leland E. Bryant, 1750-1754 Serrano Avenue

25) You are now entering "stucco-box apartment land," where many of the nondescript apartment buildings have names. Builders did this to try to elevate the status of the lowly apartment building, so "The Russell Rivera," "The Park Western," and "The Corsair" were some of the names given to these structures.

Look to your left and you will see the real gem of the neighborhood, another structure designed in the French Chateauesque style. It is called "The Trianon," after Marie Antoinette's castle in France, however, it actually looks more like the Chateau D'Azay-Le-Rideau, also in France and built in 1516. Architect Leland Bryant designed other Chateauesque structures in Los Angeles, and he also designed the Art Deco Argyle Hotel (formerly Sunset Tower) on the Sunset Strip in West Hollywood. This location is listed as Historic-Cultural Monument #616 by the City of Los Angeles.

Turn left on Loma Linda Avenue

26) This house on the corner of Loma Linda Avenue and Harvard Drive is an anomaly in this neighborhood of stucco box apartment buildings. Designed in the Greek Revival style of Victorian architecture, characterized by the triangular pediment rooflines, columns with scrolled capitals, and dentil molding, which look like teeth, this wood house was probably built around 1907. It was the home of James R. Toberman, uncle of real estate developer Charles Toberman, and once-mayor of Los Angeles. A search for an original building permit turned up nothing, but the wood siding is one of the clues to its date. It has definitely seen better days, but worth noting to show what was here nearly one hundred years ago.

26) James R. Toberman House, c. 1907, (architect unknown), 1749 North Harvard Drive

Turn left on Harvard Drive Right on Franklin Avenue

27) Graham ("Wedgwood") House, 1917, Frank L.Meline, 5137 Franklin Avenue

27) Look to the left to see the blue and white house on the hill, which resembles Wedgwood China. Another example of combining various architectural styles, the fluted columns are Neo-Classical, the shutters are "Colonial-esque," and the quoins on the corners and bracketed overhanging roof are from the Italian Renaissance style. Of course, the terra cotta roof tiles are Mediterranean, but here are painted green. Somehow they all come together to create a coherent design. The builder Frank Meline was responsible for the construction of many residences in southern California.

Continue slowly on Franklin Avenue

28) Just two houses down from the "Wedgwood" house is a remarkable home designed by the son of Frank Lloyd Wright, Frank Lloyd Wright, Jr. or Lloyd Wright, as he was known. Called the "Jaws" house because of its enormous front opening that looks like the jaws of an enormous animal, this house uses the concept of the textile block, (first brought forth by Frank Lloyd Wright and seen later on this tour in the Ennis-Brown House), as decoration. The front entrance is just below the "jaws" opening, and a stairway takes you around to end up right in front of the window. The arrangement here is that of a central open courtyard with the rooms of the house surrounding it. In the courtyard is a swimming pool, so the backyard is really in the middle of the house. Built originally for John and Ruth Sowden, they wanted a "showplace" house for entertaining. It was completely restored in 2002. This house is listed on the National Register of Historic Places.

Born in 1890, Frank Lloyd Wright, Jr. was the oldest of Wright's six children and also an architect. He worked in Boston at the offices of Frederick Law Olmstead, the landscape designer of Central Park and many other urban parks. He studied landscaping and the relationship between houses and their landscaped environments. He came to Los Angeles in 1913 and worked on many of his father's projects including the Hollyhock House (seen later on this tour). Los Angeles, being the center of the movie industry, gave him an opportunity to work briefly at Paramount Studios as a set designer. He designed many houses in Los Angeles, but his best known structure is the Wayfarer's Chapel in Palos Verdes, south of L.A. It is a masterpiece in glass and wood overlooking the Pacific Ocean. His own home is on Doheny Drive in West Hollywood. He died in 1978.

28) Sowden ("Jaws") House, 1926, Lloyd Wright, Jr., 5121 FRANKLIN AVENUE

Turn left on Vermont Avenue

29) On your right, the white building with the gold onion domes on top is the Sikh Temple. It is a place of worship for the religious sect of Hinduism called Sikhism founded in the 16th century.

29) Gurdwara Vermont Sikh Temple, 1996, Concept Technology, Inc., 1966 NORTH VERMONT AVENUE

Continue on Vermont Avenue

30) Coming up on your right is a Catholic church and school, in sharp contrast to the Sikh Temple. It is a fairly typical design for church architecture of the 1960s and uses split-face brick extensively.

30) Our Mother of Good Counsel Catholic Church and School, 1960, Anthony A. Kauzor, 2060 North Vermont Avenue

Continue on Vermont Avenue Cross Los Feliz Blvd.

31) You are now entering Griffith Park; at nearly 4,000 acres it is one of the largest urban parks in America. It is named after Colonel Griffith Jenkins Griffith who purchased the property for $50,000. In the 1880s, he donated the park to the City of Los Angeles. Griffith had worked and made his fortune in mining and he was also an officer with the California National Guard. He was a tempestuous alcoholic and in a drunken rage shot his wife in the eye after jealousy overcame his emotions. He was imprisoned at San Quentin Penitentiary for two years.

Within the grounds of Griffith Park are various areas for specific activities. A golf course, tennis courts, horse stables, a Boy Scout camp, the Gene Autry Museum of Western Heritage, the Los Angeles Zoo, Travel Town – which houses a collection of antique trains – a carousel, a children's train, a bird sanctuary, miles of hiking trails, acres of parklands, and picnic grounds all are enclosed within the boundaries of Griffith Park, as are the Greek Theater and the Griffith Observatory and Planetarium.

The Greek Theater is an outdoor concert venue that was designed as a Greek amphitheater. It is a relatively small venue and every seat has excellent sight lines to the stage. It was recently renovated in 2004.

31) Griffith Park, Vermont Canyon Road

Follow the park road through the tunnel all the way to the Observatory.

32) Griffith Observatory and Planetarium, 1935, John C. Austin and F.M. Ashley, Restoration and Expansion, (projected completion 2005), Hardy Holzman Pfeiffer Associates, and Levin and Associates, 2800 East Observatory Road

32) Designed in the Late Art Deco style with the geometrical streamlining popular in the 1930s, it also has some Greek design ornamentation, such as the fret pattern seen in the border motif. It is symmetrical in layout with a large central copper dome, which houses the planetarium and two smaller flanking domes, where the telescopes are located. An obelisk on the front lawn honors ancient astronomers Galileo, Copernicus, and others. The observatory was closed in 2003 for a major restoration and expansion and is scheduled to reopen in 2005. "Rebel Without a Cause," the movie starring James Dean and Natalie Wood was filmed here. It is listed as Historic-Cultural Monument #168 by the City of Los Angeles.

Go back down the way you came
Pass the Greek Theater
Turn right on Cromwell Avenue
Right on Glendower Avenue
Continue winding around on Glendower
Just after Bryn Mawr Drive...

33) Look to the left at the grey house with the green fiberglass fence in front. This was designed by Austrian-born architect Rudolf M. Schindler who worked with Frank Lloyd Wright in Chicago. Wright sent him here to work on the Hollyhock House (seen later) and he lived in Los Angeles for the rest of his life. He died in 1953. This house was built towards the end of his career for Samuel Skolnik. Unfortunately, it is difficult to see from the street, but it is possible to see the geometric forms he used, the curving of the retaining wall, and clerestory windows. He used lots of glass here – even a glass pitched roof in the kitchen – to take advantage of this high point with magnificent city views.

33) Skolnik House, 1952, R.M. Schindler, 2567 Glendower Avenue

Continue up the street

34) Here on your left is a masterpiece designed by Frank Lloyd Wright. Known as the Ennis-Brown House, it was named for the original owners, Charles and Mabel Ennis, who had a clothing store in Downtown Los Angeles, and for Augustus Brown, who bought, lived in, and maintained the house from the 1960s until his death in 2000. No one is certain why the Ennis' hired Frank Lloyd Wright, in particular, to design their house, but it was the last and the largest of the four "textile block" houses he designed in the Los Angeles area. This house is close to 10,000 square feet in area and is built of approximately 24,000 "textile blocks," as Wright called them. The blocks are made of decomposed granite that was taken from and also manufactured on this location. The concrete was poured into a patterned mold and then the blocks were "strung" together with steel reinforcing rod. Wright felt strongly that a house should relate to its environment and he thought that the concrete block was an appropriate material to use in the southwest. Wright hoped that the blocks could be mass-produced and allow people to create inexpensive homes of their own. That never occurred; however, this house stands as a testament of ingenuity and innovation. Said to be inspired by ancient Mayan architecture by some, the central block form does bear resemblance to Mayan temples and strongly asserts itself on the steep hill with sweeping views of the city below. The house is entered through a dark, compressed doorway and then gradually opens up with the main rooms, living and dining, opening up to the views with patterned leaded glass windows. The kitchen and bedrooms are typically small but efficient. As the house exists now, there are some design elements that are not as he wanted. Wright ended up walking off the job before it was finished due to conflicts with the clients, something he did more than once during his career. Over the years, the house has fallen into disrepair and the impact of the 1994 6.8 Northridge Earthquake resulted in significant damage. The Ennis-Brown House has been used in numerous films, including *The House on Haunted Hill*, *Blade Runner*, *Day of the Locusts*, *Black Rain*, *Rush Hour*, and others, as well as many still-photo shoots. It now belongs to the Trust for Preservation of Cultural Heritage, a non-profit organization which overseas the operations and maintenance of the house. It is listed as Historic-Cultural Monument #149 by the City of Los Angeles, is on the National Register of Historic Places, as well as the 2004 list of the 100 Most Endangered Sites by the World Monuments Fund. Restoration was underway in 2003 with grandson Eric Lloyd Wright involved in the project.

34) Ennis-Brown House, 1924, Frank Lloyd Wright, 2607 and 2655 Glendower Avenue

Turn around
Go back down the hill all the way
Turn left on Los Feliz Blvd.

35) Just past the intersection of Los Feliz Blvd. and Vermont Avenue, quickly look to your left and you will see the striking Los Feliz Manor apartment building built five years after the Ennis-Brown House. The building possesses a similar Mayan expression, but with more of an Art Deco sensibility, complete with turquoise terra cotta block decoration. In the smaller apartments in this building, Murphy beds come out of the walls as space savers.

35) Los Feliz Manor Apartments, 1929, Jack Grundfor, 4643 Los Feliz Blvd.

Continue on Los Feliz Blvd.

36) The Derby/Louise's Trattoria, 1991, (former location of the Brown Derby Restaurant), 4500 Los Feliz Blvd.

36) Look to your right at the Italian restaurant on the corner of Hillhurst Avenue. This was the location of one of the four original Brown Derby Restaurants. There was one in Beverly Hills, one on Wilshire Blvd. across from the Ambassador Hotel, one at Hollywood and Vine, and one here. Just before Louise's Trattoria acquired the building in the early 1990s, it was a restaurant called Michael's and had a flat dropped interior ceiling, concealing the dome shape. The new restaurant design restored the original flattened dome and the nightclub on the side was named "The Derby," in honor of what was on this location many years earlier.

Turn right on Hillhurst Avenue
Right on Clayton Avenue
Left on Lyman Place
Right on Hollywood Blvd.

Map Three

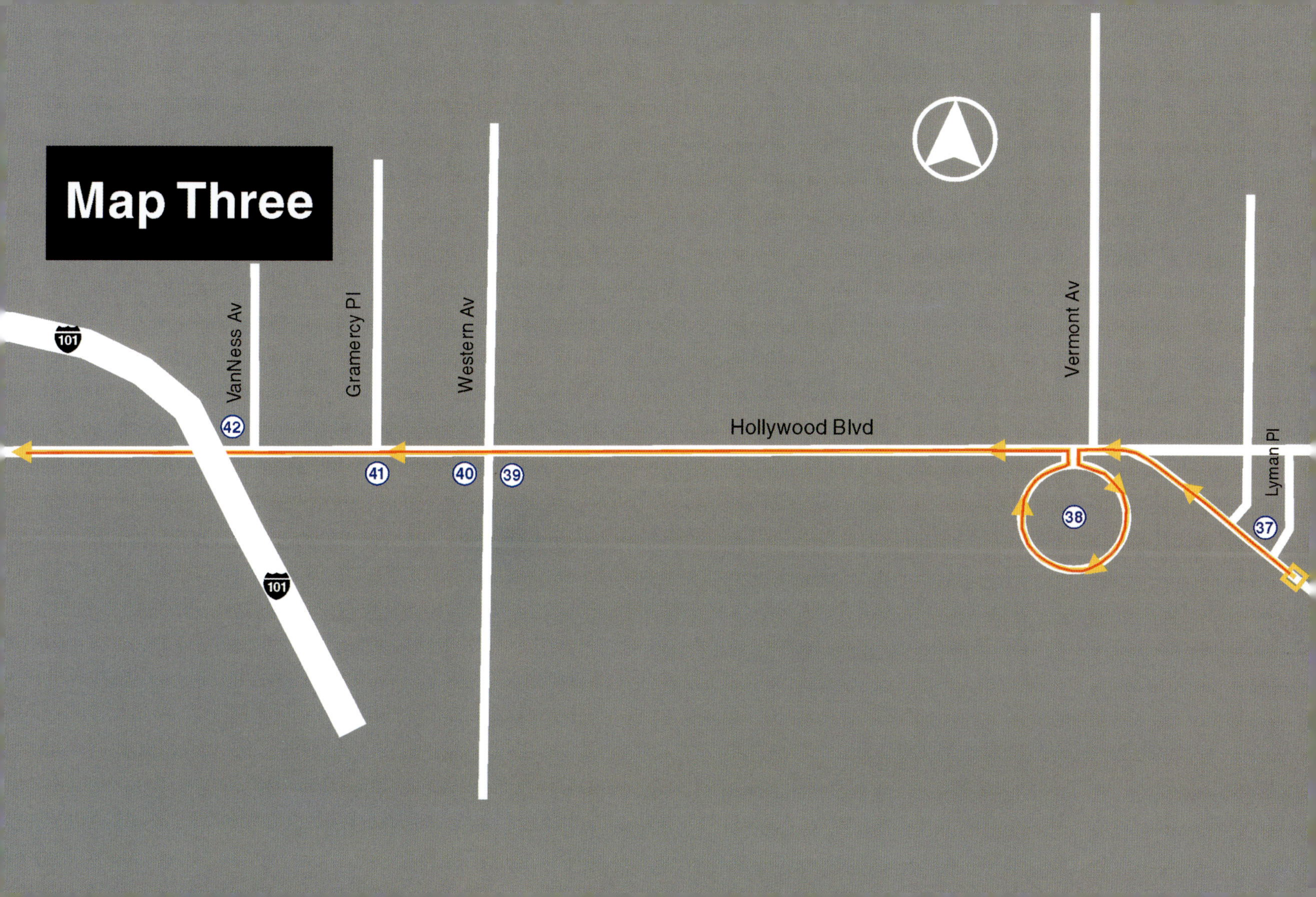

101
VanNess Av
Gramercy Pl
Western Av
Vermont Av
Hollywood Blvd
Lyman Pl
42
41
40
39
38
37

37) This structure here on your right was designed by local architect William Dale Brantley and is an attractive example of Post-modern architecture. Most of the technology of the building, including the structural I-beams painted yellow, the ductwork, the insulation, etc., has been left exposed. The idea is the glorification of technology and industrial materials, and the concept that a building is more interesting in the process of construction rather than when it is covered over by walls. The large glass windows provide a great view from the street to see all that the architect wants you to see on the inside.

37) Goodwill Industries Thrift Store and Donation Center, 1999, aARt.s (William Dale Brantley), 4575 Hollywood Blvd.

Continue on Hollywood Blvd.
Pass Vermont Avenue
Turn left into Barnsdall Art Park and follow the driveway
Turn left at the Hollyhock House driveway

38) The Barnsdall Art Park was named after Aline Barnsdall, a wealthy oil heiress and arts patron. She envisioned an "art park" of sorts and commissioned Frank Lloyd Wright to build a house for her here, as well as other buildings for arts activities. Wright began building the house on Olive Hill in 1917. This house was built of tilt-up concrete with slightly canted walls. The hollyhock flower, Aline Barnsdall's favorite flower, was abstracted and geometrized by Wright and used as a design motif throughout. Evidence of this can be seen in the border pattern around the roof and on the planters. Now it can also be seen in the lampposts around the property which have been restored. Barnsdall and Wright had terrible arguments over the house and Wright sent R.M. Schindler from Chicago to supervise construction and to finish it. (Luckily for us, Schindler never went back to Chicago, instead settling and building great architecture here!) Barnsdall only lived in the house for a few years, citing leaking roofs and a heavy concrete front door she had trouble opening as reasons for her exit. Fortunately, she donated the house and grounds to the city in 1927 to be used as an art park, as it has been ever since. Tours of the house had always been available until the house was deemed unsafe after damage sustained by the 1994 6.8 Northridge Earthquake. Currently, restoration has been halted. Other buildings on the grounds, such as Residence A, which is behind you at the bend of the road, was supposedly designed by R.M. Schindler, and originally intended to be a visiting artist's residence. It has served as the location of adult art classes since the 1940s. It has also been closed for restoration since 2002 and not yet reopened. Barnsdall Art Park is listed as Historic-Cultural Monument #34 by the City of Los Angeles. The Hollyhock House is listed as Historic-Cultural Monument #12 by the City of Los Angeles. Residence A is listed as Historic-Cultural Monument #33 by the City of Los Angeles. This location is also listed on the National Register of Historic Places.

38) Hollyhock House (Barnsdall Art Park), Residence A, 1917-1921, Frank Lloyd Wright, 4800 Hollywood Blvd.

Continue driving around the loop driveway Look to your left...

The Junior Arts Center, an art school for children, was built by the city in 1967 and the large white building is where the art gallery with auditorium below was built in 1971.

Continue down the driveway Turn left on Hollywood Blvd.

You are now driving through Little Armenia and Thai Town, portions of East Hollywood so named for their large populations of Armenian and Thai residents.

39) Here on the left, on the southeast corner of Hollywood Blvd. and Western Avenue, is an apartment building built directly above the Hollywood and Western Metro subway station. Of rectilinear form and painted in the same bright colors as the polychromatic-tile entrance of the underground subway, it was designed as low-income housing. Commissioned by McCormick, Therin & Salazar, there are sixty units and a central courtyard, with retail spaces on the ground floor and apartments above. This was very complex to build because of its siting above a subway station. The colorful graphic quality of the exterior paint scheme makes the entire building very attractive and energetic, reflecting the motion of the busy intersection.

39) Hollywood/Western Apartments, 2003, Kanner Architects, 1672 Western Avenue, Subway Station, 5450 Hollywood Blvd.

40) Louis B. Mayer Building (Central Casting), 1928, S. Charles Lee, 5504 Hollywood Blvd.

40) Again on the left, on the southwest corner of Hollywood Blvd. and Western Avenue, is a building from the late 1920s. It was home to the Association of Motion Picture Producers and Central Casting. Many Hollywood business meetings and auditions took place here, also serving as a location in the movie *Double Indemnity* with Barbara Stanwyck. Louis B. Mayer, founder of Metro-Goldwyn-Mayer (MGM) movie studios financed the construction of the building, whose architect was known for the design of other structures such as the Max Factor Building on Highland Avenue just south of Hollywood Blvd. (seen later on the tour), the Tower Theater, and Los Angeles Theater in Downtown L.A. Most remarkable here is the relief sculpture adorning the building and fire escapes, depicting scenes from the silent screen era. Look closely to see a director sitting in a canvas director's chair and holding a cone-shaped megaphone, camera operators, and actors in dramatic poses. The building had fallen into terrible disrepair, and after housing Hollywood Billiards in the basement, it was condemned due to further damage caused by the 1994 6.8 Northridge Earthquake. Following that it was home to drug dealers and squatters, until it was finally restored beautifully in the late 1990s. This location is listed as Historic-Cultural Monument #336 by the City of Los Angeles.

41) Here on your left, a little, big building designed by the same architects who designed Bullock's Wilshire Department store on Wilshire Blvd. and Union Station Downtown. With the tall tower looking like a mini Empire State Building, this was originally a bank, and many years later its interior was remodeled by Josh Schweitzer of Schweitzer BIM for a film production company. It now houses the offices of another film production company. The building was also used in the movie *L.A. Confidential* as a movie theater.

41) Bank Building, 1931, John and Donald Parkinson, 5620 Hollywood Blvd.

42) Here on the right, on the corner of Hollywood Blvd. and Van Ness Avenue, is a church built in the early 1960s. The building is of beautiful curvilinear form featuring square stained glass windows that filter colored light into the Sanctuary, and walls clad in tiny mosaic tiles that change colors when exposed to light. Walls of the church not exposed to sunlight are actually whitish in color.

42) Hollywood Seventh Day Adventist Church, 1961, Robert Burman, 1711 North Van Ness Avenue

If you look to your right near the corner of Hollywood Blvd. and Gower Street, you will get a good view of the Capitol Records Tower.

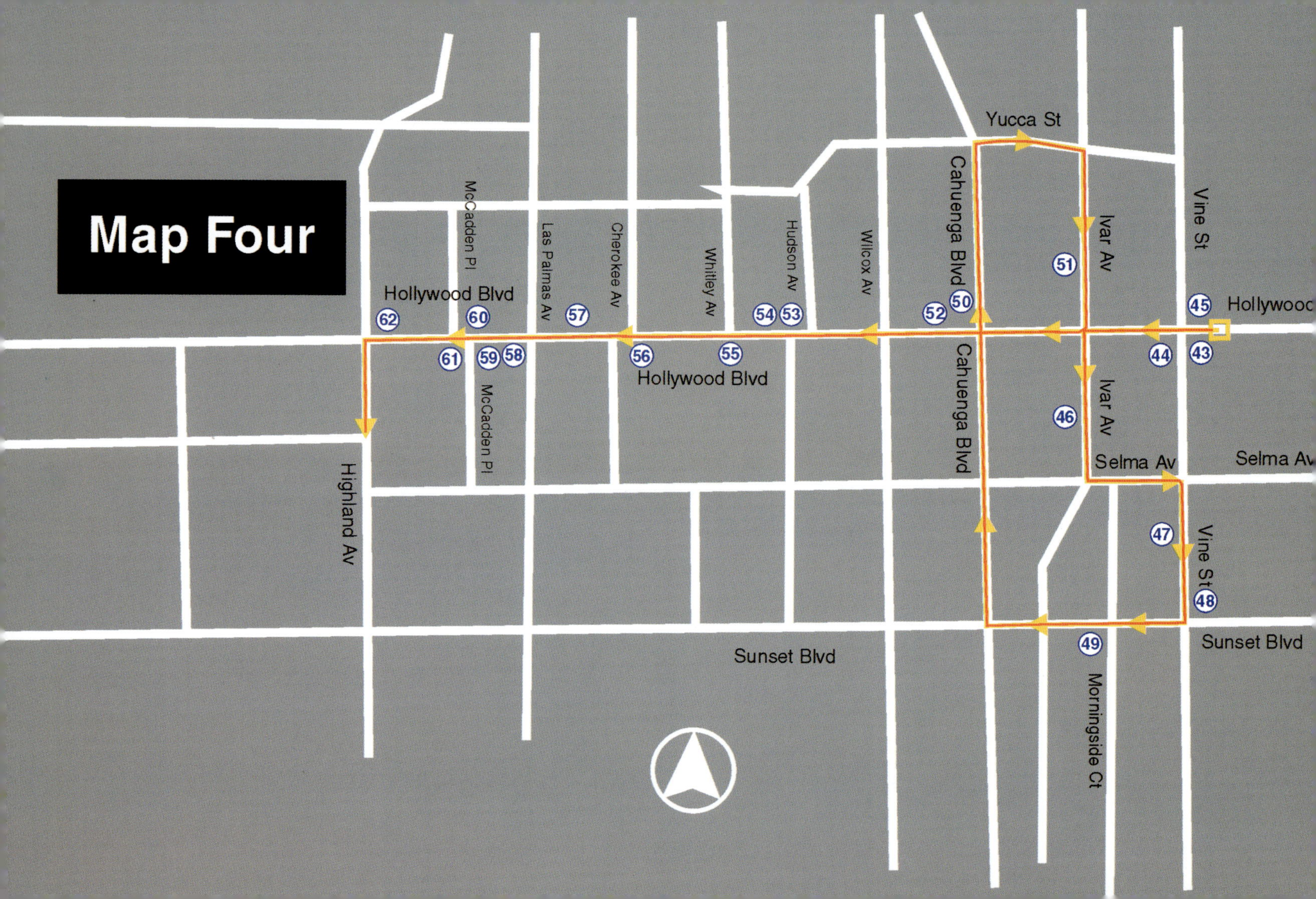
Map Four
Yucca St
Cahuenga Blvd
Ivar Av
Vine St
Hollywood
McCadden Pl
Las Palmas Av
Cherokee Av
Whitley Av
Hudson Av
Wilcox Av
Hollywood Blvd
Hollywood Blvd
Highland Av
McCadden Pl
Cahuenga Blvd
Ivar Av
Selma Av
Selma Av
Vine St
Sunset Blvd
Sunset Blvd
Morningside Ct
43
44
45
46
47
48
49
50
51
52
53
54
55
56
57
58
59
60
61
62

43) On the southeast corner of Hollywood Blvd. and Vine Street is the building that originally housed the Academy of Motion Picture Arts and Sciences, now located in Beverly Hills. That's the Academy Awards people, as in, "I'd like to thank the Academy…" This was one of the reasons for the popularity of the Hollywood and Vine corner. Loosely based on the Italian Renaissance commercial style, with its columns and crowning cornice with modillion brackets at the roof, it also housed the offices of Charlie Chaplin and other notables from the movie industry. This was Hollywood's first high-rise building. This location is listed as Historic-Cultural Monument #666 by the City of Los Angeles and is included in the Hollywood Boulevard Commercial and Entertainment District.

44) On the southwest corner of Hollywood and Vine was a Broadway department store, another magnet for activity at this corner that now houses offices. Also designed in the Italian Renaissance commercial style, it was part of a chain of now defunct department stores. Further down on Vine Street is the Plaza Hotel, where actors including Doris Day lived at one time or another, and another reason for the popularity of this corner. This location is listed as Historic-Cultural Monument #664 by the City of Los Angeles and is included in the Hollywood Boulevard Commercial and Entertainment District.

43) Taft Building, 1923, Walker & Eisen, 6290 Hollywood Blvd.

44) The Broadway Building, 1927, Fred Dorn, 1938, John and Donald Parkinson, 6300 Hollywood Blvd.

45) The tall building on the northeast corner of Hollywood and Vine was beautifully restored in early 2001. The building that once housed offices will now house apartments, as the building's redevelopment is currently in the planning stages. Adorned with shield shapes and gargoyles, and of massive rounded block form, it combines elements of the Art Deco, Neo-Gothic, and Egyptian Revival in its block massing. This location is included in the Hollywood Boulevard Commercial and Entertainment District.

On the northwest corner, the green building, now home to a nightclub, was originally a Sardi's restaurant designed by R.M. Schindler. However, it was remodeled beyond recognition.

45) The Equitable Building, 1929, Aleck Curlett, 6263 Hollywood Blvd.

Turn left on Ivar Avenue

46) Here on your right is the Hollywood Branch Library. Designed by the same architect who designed Walt Disney Concert Hall in Downtown L.A., the exterior composition is a symmetrical arrangement of sculptural cube forms. The large, central, glass-fronted box is flanked by toppling glass boxes on either side. Gehry creates a very light space inside through the use of the skylights. The interior features a circular stairwell leading up to the second floor to an open, spacious reading and reference area. The blue ceramic "bathroom" tiles are indicative of Gehry's penchant for using materials in unexpected applications. This library was named after the wife of Samuel Goldwyn, one of the founders of Metro-Goldwyn-Mayer (MGM) movie studios. She was the president of the Samuel Goldwyn Foundation, which donated funds for the library to be built.

46) Frances Howard Goldwyn Hollywood Regional Library, 1985, Frank O. Gehry, 1623 Ivar Avenue

Left on Selma Avenue Right on Vine Street

47) Here on your right is a new complex with a mixture of concepts. An existing historic structure on the site, the TAV Building and the original neon sign for Schwab's Drug Store (originally located elsewhere) on the Vine Street side have been incorporated into the new design. This is also a mixed-use building with retail shops on the ground floor and apartments above.

47) Sunset-Vine Complex, 2004, Roschen Van Cleve Architects, 1501 North Vine Street

48) Across the street, here on the left corner of Sunset and Vine is what is now the Washington Mutual Bank, originally a Home Savings and Loan Bank. All of the Home Savings and Loan Bank buildings were designed by Millard Sheets. They were all of box form, clad with travertine tile, and adorned with a central mosaic usually depicting something particular to each area. In this case, the movie industry is depicted in the mosaic. There is actually a listing of actor's names embedded into the walls. This is also a historic site because the director Cecil B. De Mille filmed the movie *The Squaw Man* in the horse barn (seen later on the tour) that was originally located here. After that it was the site of the West Coast NBC Radio City, from where many radio programs, including *Amos 'n' Andy* and *Jack Benny*, were broadcast. A new building was built to house the bank. A private museum housing memorabilia from NBC's radio days is located underground.

48) Home Savings and Loan (now Washington Mutual Bank), c. 1950s, Millard Sheets, 1500 North Vine Street

Turn right on Sunset Blvd.

49) Look to your left at the corner of Sunset Blvd. and Ivar Avenue and you will see the white geodesic dome of the original Cinerama Dome Theater. This theater, which was saved by the Los Angeles Conservancy in the late 1990s, has the distinction of being the only concrete geodesic dome in the world. Its design was based on Buckminster Fuller's development of the geodesic dome structure. It is seventy feet tall and comprised of 316 individual panels. This method of construction was very efficient and inexpensive compared to other theater construction costs. The hope was that this would be the model for the construction of other theaters built to show films made in the Cinerama process, shot with three cameras and shown with three projectors. The Cinerama Dome Theater opened in 1963 with the movie *It's a Mad, Mad, Mad, Mad World*. The Arclight Cinerama Dome Entertainment Center complex augmented this location in 2002, adding more theaters, a restaurant, and shops where the parking lot once was. This location is listed as Historic-Cultural Monument #659 by the City of Los Angeles.

49) Cinerama Dome Theater (now Arclight), 1963, Welton Becket and Associates, 6360 Sunset Blvd.

Turn right on Cahuenga Blvd.
Pass Hollywood Blvd.
Turn left into the second driveway of the Greyhound Bus station

50) The green and blue stucco box was built recently. The small, square, cutout windows, some with glass and some without, pierce the back wall, while the front features a floor-to-ceiling glass wall. The small scale of the building has a very open and contemporary feel to it. Greyhound wanted to update their image, achieved in one way by the cutout greyhound dog logo separated from the building and placed high on a pole. Although the logo is separated from the building, it actually has a stronger presence because of it. This location was also the site of the mansion built in 1901 by the French-born artist Paul DeLongpre, after which a street in Hollywood is named, and whose paintings still sell today.

50) Greyhound Bus Station, 1999, Josh Schweitzer, Schweitzer/BIM, 1715 North Cahuenga Blvd.

Continue around the parking lot
Turn left on Cahuenga Blvd.
Right on Yucca Street
Right on Ivar Avenue

51) Knickerbocker Hotel, 1929, John M. Cooper, 1714 Ivar Avenue

51) Here on your left, this hotel was once a glamorous gathering place, and is now an apartment building for senior citizens. It was designed in a very spare version of the Italian Renaissance style, with a flat roof and crowning cornice with modillion brackets and scrolling, and foliage and shield shape decoration above the central window. Architect Paul Williams designed alterations and additions in 1935 and 1954. This hotel's historical significance is based on the people who lived and died here. Rudolph Valentino frequented the hotel's bar, as did Marilyn Monroe and Joe DiMaggio. Frances Farmer, the disturbed actress, had a mental breakdown in her hotel room; costume designer Irene Gibbons jumped from the eleventh floor after slitting her wrists; D.W. Griffith, the silent film director, was at the hotel when he died from a cerebral hemorrhage; and William Frawley, of *I Love Lucy* fame, died on the sidewalk outside the hotel. Elvis Presley was also a hotel guest, but didn't die here! The television show *Queen for a Day* was broadcast from this hotel. This location is included in the Hollywood Boulevard Commercial and Entertainment District.

Turn right on Hollywood Blvd.

52) On the right, where the two steel towers are on top of the building, was originally the Warner Theater, which was most recently the Pacific Movie Theater, and is currently the location of a private film editing screening room. It was designed in a version of the European Beaux-Arts style. This location is listed as Historic-Cultural Monument #572 by the City of Los Angeles, and is included in the Hollywood Boulevard Commercial and Entertainment District.

52) Warner Brothers Theater, Pacific Theater (now ETC, Entertainment Technology Center), 1928, G. Albert Lansburgh, 6433 Hollywood Blvd.

53) Here on your right is a restoration project that has restored the apartment building that once housed actors. Some of the landlords in the early days of Hollywood would post signs that said, "No actors, no dogs." Financed by Samuel Goldwyn and Jesse Lasky of the Lasky-DeMille Players, they knew that actors whose salaries might be uncertain needed a place to live. Built in the Mediterranean style, the Hillview was damaged by the 1994 6.8 Northridge Earthquake and then a fire a few years later. It has once again become one of the few residences in the commercial district of Hollywood Blvd. This location is included in the Hollywood Boulevard Commercial and Entertainment District

53) Hillview Apartments, 1917, Tifal Brothers, Restoration 2004, Roschen Van Cleve Architects, 6531 Hollywood Blvd.

54) Right here, set back from the street next to the Hillview Apartments, is the oldest single family residence remaining on Hollywood Blvd. The Shingle style Victorian house was home to the Janes sisters who ran a school here. There were other residences on Hollywood Blvd. that were built during the turn of the century, but none remain. This location is listed as Historic-Cultural Monument #227 by the City of Los Angeles and is included in the Hollywood Boulevard Commercial and Entertainment District.

54) Janes House, 1903, Dennis & Farwell, 6541 Hollywood Blvd.

55) Look to your left for an example of the exuberant Art Deco style of the Frederick's lingerie store in shades of purple, lavender, and pink. Frederick Mellinger started with a department store and turned it into a store specializing in lingerie. Make sure to see the Lingerie Museum in the back of the store. Also, notice the Art Deco Toy Store next door. This location is included in the Hollywood Boulevard Commercial and Entertainment District.

55) S.H. Kress Department Store (now Frederick's of Hollywood), 1935, Edward F. Sibbert, 6608 Hollywood Blvd.

56) Here on the left side of the street, at the southwest corner of Hollywood Blvd. and Cherokee Avenue is a tall, white building in the Art Deco style. It once housed the Screen Actors Guild and the Writer's Guild, both now located in Beverly Hills. Currently, this building is another example of the architectural restoration going on in Hollywood. Just above the first floor notice the metal decorative border which has recently been revealed. For many years this was covered over by signage, and now, because of the resurgence of interest in historical architectural styles, the signage has been removed to reveal the original architectural details of the 1920s.

56) Hollywood Center Building, c. 1925, (architect unknown), 1655 Cherokee Ave.

57) On the right, with the green sign above the building is the oldest continuously operating restaurant in Hollywood. Architecturally nondescript on the exterior, the building is warm and very "Old-Hollywood" on the interior. Some of the waiters have been there for over thirty years. Specialties are martinis and Caesar salads. This location is included in the Hollywood Boulevard Commercial and Entertainment District.

57) Musso & Frank Grill, 1917, L.A. Smith, 6667 Hollywood Blvd.

58) Here on the left is the site of the very first Hollywood movie premier. *Robin Hood*, starring Douglas Fairbanks, was the movie that opened this theater to great success. Meyer and Holler, also known as the Milwaukee Building Company, were real estate developers and had Raymond Kennedy, an architect in their firm, design the theater. The Egyptian theme was exotic and in line with the Art Deco style of the 1920s. King Tut's tomb was discovered the same year this theater was built.

58) Egyptian Theater, 1922, Meyer & Holler, Restored 1998, Hodgetts & Fung, 6712 Hollywood Blvd.

Charles Toberman made the initial investment to have the theater built, and hired promoter Sid Grauman to run it. Toberman also invested in the Chinese Theater, the El Capitan Theater, and the Roosevelt Hotel all just up the street. Hollywood Blvd. and the surrounding businesses had deteriorated in the 1960s and 1970s and the theater finally closed in 1992. However, it was purchased by the American Cinematheque from the City of Los Angeles, providing that it would be restored and remain a theater. It was fully restored by the firm Hodgetts & Fung with preservation architect Peyton Hall of Historic Resources Group, and re-opened in 1998. The American Cinematheque showcases film festivals and themed screenings, and is open to the public for viewing films and for tours. This location is listed as Historic-Cultural Monument #584 by the City of Los Angeles and is included in the Hollywood Boulevard Commercial and Entertainment District.

59) Just next door to the Egyptian Theater is the Pig 'N Whistle restaurant, a family place with a soda fountain that originally opened in 1927. It was part of a national chain and this structure was last a fast-food pizza joint before it was fully restored in 2001 and opened as a family restaurant with a British-themed menu, although in the later hours of the night it has more of a nightclub clientele. The façade was taken down and the original carved wood details of 1927 were revealed. The dancing pig still graces the interior from the original, although many of the furnishings were sold off to the restaurant down the street. This location is included in the Hollywood Boulevard Commercial and Entertainment District.

Both the Egyptian Theater and the Pig 'N Whistle restaurant are excellent examples of the restoration Renaissance of Hollywood.

59) Pig 'N Whistle Restaurant, 1927, Morgan, Walls & Clements, 6714 Hollywood Blvd.

60) Here on your right, across the street, is what is now The Erotic Museum, opened in 2004 and showcasing exhibitions on human sexuality. Originally, the Spanish Colonial Revival style storefront housed Otto Dit's tailor shop, and on the second floor the Hollywood-Maxwell Company, a lingerie shop that sold things like garters, corsets, and brassieres. After the tailor and lingerie shop were gone, a number of bookstores occupied this space, and just before the museum moved in it was a Hollywood souvenir shop. For many years, the intricate surface decoration of the exterior was completely covered over with signage, but when the new museum began remodeling, they discovered the beautiful decoration and decided to expose it again, restoring as much of it as they could. Notice the shield shapes, scrolling, foliage, and heroic busts in the decoration, all elements of the Spanish Colonial Revival style.

60) Tailor Shop/Hollywood-Maxwell Company (now The Erotic Museum), 1926, Morgan, Walls & Clements, 6741 Hollywood Blvd.

Directly next to the museum is another example of a 1920s Art Deco style building's details being revealed after being covered over for many years. This all contributes to the restoration Renaissance of Hollywood! This location is included in the Hollywood Boulevard Commercial and Entertainment District.

61) On your left, the large brick building, which is now the Scientology Test Center, was originally Hollywood's first luxury hotel. It was owned by brothers Al and Charles Christie, who were the first to open a movie studio in Hollywood – the Nestor Studios. They had this built in the English Georgian style and this was the first hotel to have bathrooms within the individual rooms. This location is included in the Hollywood Boulevard Commercial and Entertainment District.

61) The Christie Hotel (now Scientology Test Center), 1922, Arthur B. Kelley, 6724 Hollywood Blvd.

62) On the northeast corner of Hollywood Blvd. and Highland Avenue is the First National Bank Building. It was built by the same builders as the Egyptian and Chinese Theaters, and is very theatrical as it addresses the intersection with its cylinder-shaped corner with a conical top. Swag forms and medallions add to the elegant presence of the building, as well as decorative relief sculpture. The structure steps down as it tapers down both streets. It is a hybrid combination of the elegant Art Deco style and French Chateauesque. When it was built, it was the tallest building in Hollywood. It has housed offices for years. This location is included in the Hollywood Boulevard Commercial and Entertainment District.

62) Los Angeles First National Bank Building, 1927, Meyer & Holler, 6777 Hollywood Blvd.

Map Five

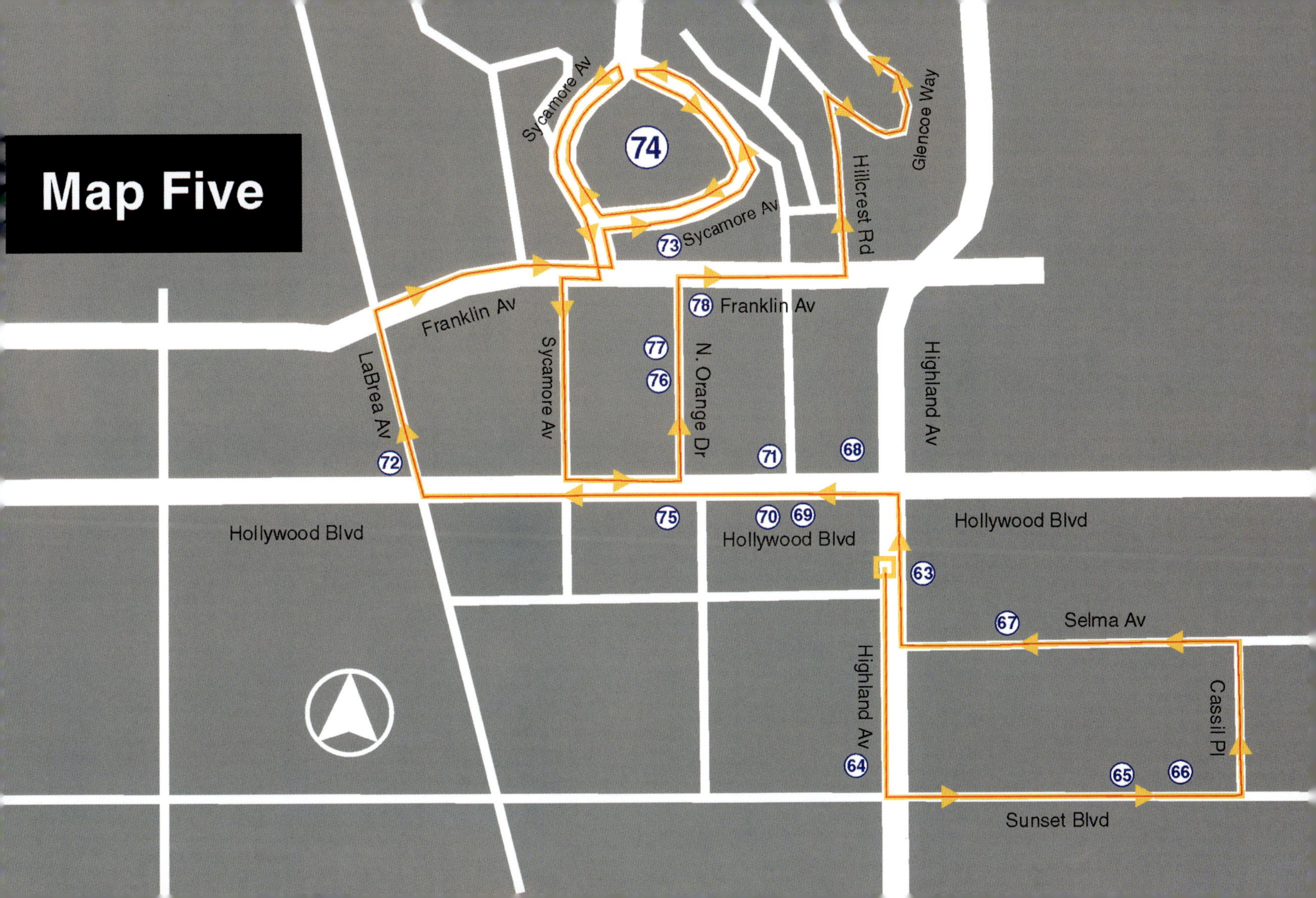

74
Sycamore Av
Glencoe Way
Hillcrest Rd
73 Sycamore Av
Franklin Av
78 Franklin Av
77
76
LaBrea Av
Sycamore Av
N. Orange Dr
Highland Av
72
71
68
75
70
69
Hollywood Blvd
Hollywood Blvd
Hollywood Blvd
63
67
Selma Av
Highland Av
Cassil Pl
64
65
66
Sunset Blvd

Turn left on Highland Avenue

63) Max Factor Make-Up Salon Building, (now Hollywood History Museum), 1935, S. Charles Lee, 1660 North Highland Ave.

63) On the left side of the street is where the original location of the Max Factor make-up studio was. Factor was one of the first to develop screen make-up. It is currently a museum housing Hollywood memorabilia and an impressive collection of costumes. The building originally on this site was the Hollywood Fire and Safe Building, built around 1914 as a storage facility. Factor purchased the building in the late 1920s and architect S. Charles Lee remodeled it into an elegant salon, which opened in 1935. Lee also designed the Louis B. Mayer Building seen earlier, and a number of theaters Downtown. He designed this building in the Art Deco style with very elegant flourishes seen in the curves on the front façade, swag forms, and pink materials. Next door is a 1950s style diner. The Max Factor Make-Up Salon Building is listed as Historic-Cultural Monument #593 by the City of Los Angeles and is included in the Hollywood Boulevard Commercial and Entertainment District.

64) Here on your right is an institutional example of the Late Art Deco style called Streamline Moderne. Beautiful details, such as curved corners and leaded glass windows can be seen here as well as textile-block type of brick articulating the window frames. Because Hollywood has such a diverse population, many different languages are spoken here. Some of the more well-known alumni are Carol Burnett, John Ritter, James Garner, and Jason Robards.

64) Hollywood High School, 1935, Marsh, Smith and Powell, 1521 North Highland Avenue

Turn left on Sunset Blvd.

65) Here on the left, with the spinning globe centerpiece, is a mini-mall of sorts. Designed by the same architect of the Streamline Moderne Coca Cola Bottling Plant Downtown, it has touches of the Art Deco style. However, the concept was to create a village of storefronts and offices in various architectural styles, including English Tudor, French Provincial, Spanish Colonial Revival, and Late Art Deco Streamline Moderne. Some of the offices here are the U.S. Headquarters of Taschen art book publishers and the Hollywood Arts Council. This location is listed as Historic-Cultural Monument #134 by the City of Los Angeles. It is also listed on the National Register of Historic Places.

65) Crossroads of the World, 1935, Robert Derrah, 6671 Sunset Blvd.

66) Here on the left is a church designed in the Spanish Churrigueresque style, as it now stands. Its elaborate surface decoration of floral forms and layering is indicative of this style brought forth by Spanish architect Jose de Churriguerra in Spain. It was constructed of reinforced concrete, steel frame, and steel trusses supporting the roof. Funds had to be raised from parishioners for the construction and decoration of the church, which took many years to be completed. What you see now is the culmination of many years of construction and the work of many people. Architect J. Earl Trudeau was responsible for the wave and floral motif symbolizing water and life.

66) Church of the Blessed Sacrament, 1928, Beezer Brothers, Thomas Franklin Power-project manager, Additions and Decoration, 1954, J. Earl Trudeau, 6657 Sunset Blvd.

Turn left on Cassil Place
Left on Selma Avenue

Now visible from the back is the church and Crossroads of the World.

67) Panavision, 1996, Michael Czysz/Architropolis, 6735 Selma Avenue

67) Here on the right corner behind the fence is the location of Panavision, a supplier of movie making equipment such as cameras and lenses. This building was designed on a tight budget and with a strict program. Designed by Portland-based Architropolis, the concept was to create a highly functional building while alluding to the Hollywood film industry. The curved shape in front gives a sense of movement and energy, the pop-out windows provide a good vantage point for overseeing the daily operations of a very busy company, and the window fenestration looks like a film sprocket. The dark grey color was meant to hint at the early days of filmmaking and film noir. Function and glamour meet in one building!

Turn right on Highland Avenue
Left on Hollywood Blvd.

68) Here on the northwest corner of Hollywood Blvd. and Highland Avenue is the Hollywood and Highland Entertainment and Retail Complex, completed in 2001, and the location of the Kodak Theater, the permanent home of the Academy Awards presentations. Originally on this site was the Hollywood Hotel, a Spanish mission-inspired gathering place demolished long ago, and then home to a few nondescript shops and offices. Currently there are shops, restaurants, nightclubs, and theaters here, and underground is the Hollywood/Highland Metro subway station. The site's most notable and historic elements are the large, grey and white arch and big white elephants. They are replicas of the set designed for D.W. Griffith's 1916 silent movie *Intolerance*, which now pay homage to the movie industry in Hollywood. If you look from the right place on Hollywood Blvd. through the grey arch, you can see the HOLLYWOOD sign perfectly framed by the arch.

68) Hollywood and Highland, 2001, Ehrenkrantz, Ekstut & Kuhn; Kodak Theater, 2001, David Rockwell (Rockwell Group and Theater Project Consultants), CORNER OF HOLLYWOOD BLVD. & HIGHLAND AVENUE

69) Here on your left is another example of the restoration effort in Hollywood. Covered with circular shield shapes, it is considered to be a version of the Spanish Colonial Revival style and is strikingly bold in its surface decoration. The theater, which dates from the 1920s, was built by the same architects as the Pig 'N Whistle. The building had fallen into disrepair until The Disney Company came along in the late 1990s and restored it. They use it as a showcase for their films and sometimes have a live stage show accompaniment before the movie starts. This location is listed as Historic-Cultural Monument #495 by the City of Los Angeles and is included in the Hollywood Boulevard Commercial and Entertainment District.

69) El Capitan Theater, 1925, Morgan, Walls & Clements, G. Albert Landsburgh, 6834 Hollywood Blvd.

70) Right next to the El Capitan Theater is the Masonic Temple designed in the Neo-Classical style, after a Greek temple, with fluted columns and scrolled capitals. John C. Austin designed the Griffith Observatory as well as many other buildings in Los Angeles. The Masons are long gone from here, and this now houses a television show studio and night club. This location is listed as Historic-Cultural Monument #277 by the City of Los Angeles. It is also listed on the National Register of Historic Places.

70) Masonic Temple, 1921, John C. Austin, 6840 Hollywood Blvd.

71) Across the street on the right, designed in the Chinese style by the same builders as the Egyptian Theater, is the famous theater with the hand prints and footprints of the stars in cement. The story is that theater promoter Sid Grauman experimented within his own footprints and then immediately called silent screen star Norma Talmadge to be the first to have parts of her anatomy set in cement. Recent cement honorees include Mel Gibson, Whoopi Goldberg, and Anthony Hopkins. The site of many, many movie premiers, the first was Cecil B. DeMille's *King of Kings*. This location is listed as Historic-Cultural Monument #55 by the City of Los Angeles and is included in the Hollywood Boulevard Commercial and Entertainment District.

71) Grauman's Chinese Theater, 1927, Meyer & Holler, 6925 Hollywood Blvd.

72) On the northwest corner of Hollywood Blvd. and LaBrea Avenue is a symmetrical and serene church, built in the late 1950s with a Modern sensibility. The gently curved corner suits its location perfectly. It is a visually quiet respite from the visual cacophony of Hollywood Blvd.

In Hollywood there are many churches and places of worship. Like the extreme diversity of architecture in Los Angeles, there is almost every conceivable religious organization represented here, from Catholicism, Judaism, and Hinduism, to Sikhism, Methodist, Christian Scientist, and Scientology just to name a few.

72) The Fifth Church of Christ Scientist, 1958, Howard G. Elwell, 7107 Hollywood Blvd.

Turn right on LaBrea Avenue
Stay in right lane closest to center lane
Right on Franklin Avenue
Left on Sycamore Avenue
Continue right on Sycamore Avenue at the sign to Yamashiro's

73) As you go up the hill you will see the back of the Lane House, now known as "The Magic Castle." It was originally built as a family residence for Rollin Lane, a financier and orange grower from Redlands, a small town about an hour east of Los Angeles. Lane wanted the house to be just like Kimberly Crest, a grand house in Redlands that he admired, so he hired the same architects. (Kimberly Crest was built for the Kimberly family of Kimberly-Clark paper products.) Designed in the Chateauesque style with conical turrets, finials, and decorative railings, it is a fanciful house and in the 1960s was purchased by Milt Larsen, Bill Larsen, Jr., and the Larsen Family of Magicians, and became a private magic club for members only. The interior is Victorian in style, which was popular at the turn of the century, and incorporates stained glass windows that came from a pub in Scotland, and a wood floor from Hollywood High School. The house also features mysterious devices such as bar stools that rise and lower by themselves and a door that opens by voice command – all adding to the illusion of magic. This location is listed as Historic-Cultural Monument #406 by the City of Los Angeles.

73) Lane House (now Magic Castle), 1909, Dennis & Farwell, 7001 Franklin Avenue

Continue around the circle
Turn left into the Yamashiro Restaurant driveway

74) Originally built for Eugene and Adolph Bernheimer, collectors and dealers of Asian art. The brothers needed a place to live and house their collection. They imported Asian craftsman to build their Japanese pagoda home. The house was once in the middle of seven acres of gardens that included various varieties of trees and plants. It is located on top of a hill with wonderful views of Hollywood, and on a clear day the Pacific Ocean is visible. In 1960 it was opened as Yamashiro Japanese restaurant and remains so today.

74) Bernheimer Bungalow (now Yamashiro Restaurant), 1913, Franklin M. Small, Walter Webber, 1999 North Sycamore Avenue

Follow the driveway around
Exit to the left and down the hill out to Sycamore Drive
Right on Franklin Avenue
Quick left on Sycamore Drive
Left on Hollywood Blvd.

75) Here on your right, with the red neon sign above, is the Roosevelt Hotel in the Spanish Colonial Revival style. It is the site of the very first Academy Awards presentation that was held in 1929. This hotel is rumored to be haunted by the ghost of Marilyn Monroe. Los Angeles-based English artist David Hockney had painted blue swirls in the swimming pool; unfortunately, they were mistakenly cleaned away and are no longer visible. The hotel was also renovated and restored in the 1990s, now serving as a tourist destination. This location is listed as Historic-Cultural Monument #545 by the City of Los Angeles and is included in the Hollywood Boulevard Commercial and Entertainment District.

75) Roosevelt Hotel, 1926, Fisher, Lake & Traver, 7000 Hollywood Blvd.

Turn left on North Orange Drive

76) Look to your left at the Modern two-story apartment building. The zigzag pattern reads as a single graphic image from the side, and then as you move forward, looking straight on you can see the individual slats that serve to shade and decorate the windows. Notice the circular glass-enclosed lobby. Kenneth Lind worked in the office of R.M. Schindler at one time.

76) Hollywood Biltmore Apartments, 1957, Kenneth Lind, 1745 North Orange Drive

77) Further down on your left is a brick apartment building. Originally a hotel, it was designed in the Chinese style two years before the Chinese Theater down the street was built. Notice the Chinese motifs such as the vertical yin-yang tiles on the corners of the building, the sea horses holding up the window overhangs, and the warrior heads. Damaged by the 1994 6.8 Northridge Earthquake, it was seismically retrofit in the late 1990s.

77) The Nirvana, 1925, E.M. Erdaly, 1775 North Orange Drive

78) Next, at the southeast corner of Orange Drive and Franklin Avenue is what is now the American Society of Cinematographers (A.S.C.). Originally built as a family residence, it is one of the oldest surviving houses in the area. Designed in the Spanish Mission style after the missions that were established in California in the late 1700s, it has a Moorish-inspired cupola, or tower. The A.S.C. has been in the building since the 1930s and their initials are often seen in movie credits after the name of the Director of Photography, indicating their membership in this organization. A small camera museum with a display of antique movie cameras is also housed here.

78) Coffin Residence, (now American Society of Cinematographers), 1903, (architect unknown), 1782 North Orange Drive

Now visible from the front is the Lane House, directly in front of you.

Turn right on Franklin Ave
Left on Hillcrest Road
Right on Glencoe Way

Map Six

83
Highland Av
101
Odin St
Cahuenga Blvd
101
Wedgewood Pl
81
82
84
Milner Rd
Whitley Terrace
Hillcrest Rd
Glencoe Way
79
Orchid Av
Highland Av
Whitley Av
101
Bonita Terrace
80
Franklin Av
Franklin Av
Franklin Av
Orchid Av
Highland Av
101
Argyle Av
85

79) On your right is another textile block house built by Frank Lloyd Wright in the 1920s. These blocks have a different pattern than the Ennis-Brown House, as each of the textile block houses have their own unique pattern, and they have glass incorporated into them. Situated on the hillside with a great view of Hollywood down below, the use of glass on the view side of the house takes advantage of its siting. (The other side of this house can be seen from Franklin Avenue as it merges into Highland Avenue to the north.) The house was built for Harriet and Samuel Freeman who were forward-thinkers and interested in new ideas in architecture. Harriet Freeman was a dancer and taught dance at Hollywood High School and at Warner Brothers Studios and in her own home. Harriet Freeman was the sister of Mrs. Lovell, who lived in the Lovell Health House in the hills of Los Feliz, designed by Richard Neutra and seen on the SILVER LAKE tour. R.M. Schindler, who worked with Wright, designed some of the furniture for this house. Stipulated in the will of Harriet Freeman, the house was donated to the University of Southern California in 1986, which is in the process of restoring the house after it was badly damaged in the 1994 6.8 Northridge Earthquake. This location is listed as Historic-Cultural Monument #247 by the City of Los Angeles. It is also listed on the National Register of Historic Places.

79) Freeman House, 1924, Frank Lloyd Wright, 1962 GLENCOE WAY

Go to the end of the street and turn around
Follow Glencoe Way down
Left on Hillcrest Road
Right on Bonita Terrace
Left on Orchid Avenue
Left on Franklin Avenue

80) On your left is another church. It was designed in the English Gothic Revival style characterized by the steeply reaching, pointed arch windows and tracery decoration, diamond pane glass, and three deeply recessed wood doors in front. A tall bell tower is on the right side and the roof is composed of slate tiles. This location is listed as Historic-Cultural Monument #248 by the City of Los Angeles.

80) First United Methodist Church, 1929, Thomas B. Barber, 6817 Franklin Avenue

Stay in the extreme right lane on Franklin Avenue
Bear left onto Highland Avenue up the hill

81) Look quickly to your left and notice the box-like structure with a green pyramid roof. It is a step pyramid comprised of three block sections and adorned with shield shapes and other military regalia honoring war veterans. Swords, ribbons, and memorials to Generals Foch and Pershing make this tribute to war and patriotism complete. This location is listed as Historic-Cultural Monument #462 by the City of Los Angeles.

81) Hollywood American Legion Post 43, 1929, Weston & Weston, 2035 North Highland Avenue

82) Next on your right is a yellow structure, which is one of the oldest structures in Hollywood, and originally located near Sunset Blvd. and Vine Street. It was a barn and is also where film director Cecil B. DeMille filmed his first film, *The Squaw Man*, in 1913. The Jesse Lasky Feature Players also performed in the barn, which has been moved around quite a bit. At one time it was on the Paramount Studios lot and finally has settled here when it was deeded to Hollywood Heritage. It now houses an excellent collection of Hollywood memorabilia and is open to the public.

82) Hollywood Heritage Museum (Lasky-DeMille Barn), 1895, (architect unknown), 2100 North Highland Avenue

83) On your left, impossible to see from the street, is the open-air theater built into the mountains. It is the summer home of the Los Angeles Philharmonic Orchestra and the Hollywood Bowl Orchestra and hosts the annual Playboy Jazz Festival, many other performers including international ballets, pop and rock groups, as well as Garrison Keillor of the radio show *Prairie Home Companion*. There are over 17,000 seats, a museum, a restaurant, various snack bars, and gift shops. The tradition is to bring a picnic dinner and eat before the performance. There are many box seats where dining tables are attached to the walls and you can even bring your own bottle of wine, or dine at the restaurant on the grounds. Elaborate fireworks displays are also a frequent occurrence at the Bowl, especially on the Fourth of July. The natural terrain of the mountains creates a hollow bowl and perfect acoustics. Before the seats were put in, people would bring blankets and picnic on the grass. Various architects have designed the band shell and Myron Hunt, who designed structures throughout Los Angeles and Pasadena, designed the seating area. A trip to the bowl is well worth the experience!

83) Hollywood Bowl, 1924, 1928: Lloyd Wright, 1926: Myron Hunt (seating area), 1931: Allied Architects of Los Angeles, 1982: Frank O. Gehry, 2004: Hodgetts & Fung, 2301 North Highland Avenue

Turn right on Odin Street
Right on Cahuenga Blvd.
Right on Franklin Avenue
Right on Whitley Avenue
Follow Whitely Avenue

84) Here up in the hills is the area known as Whitley Heights. Whitley Heights was developed mostly in the 1920s after it was purchased in 1902 by H. W. Whitley, a real estate developer. The architect of the majority of the homes was A.S. Barnes, who designed in the Spanish Colonial Revival and the Mediterranean styles. This area was home to many actors including Rudolph Valentino, Gloria Swanson, Judy Garland, Tyrone Power, and Marlene Dietrich, among others. What is significant about this development is that it proved that the hillsides could be developed. This was one of the first hillside developments, and its success paved the way for the future. Whitley Heights is designated as a Historic Preservation Overlay Zone (HPOZ), which preserves the integrity of the neighborhood by having a design review board approve any exterior changes or alterations. This area is also listed on the National Register of Historic Places.

84) Various homes in Whitley Heights, c. 1920s, A.S. Barnes, Whitley Avenue

Bear right on Wedgewood Place
Right on Whitley Terrace
Right on Milner Road
Right on Highland Avenue
Right on Odin Street
Right on Cahuenga Blvd.
Left on Franklin Avenue
Pass under the Freeway
Right on Argyle Avenue

85) Here on the left behind the trees, you can just catch a glimpse of yet another church in Hollywood. Built in the 1930s in the traditional style, notice the shingled steeple. In keeping with the broadcast history of Hollywood, it was once the site of a radio broadcast of the ministry. Unfortunately, it was abandoned years ago and has not seen a congregation in a long time. This location is listed as Historic-Cultural Monument #567 by the City of Los Angeles.

85) Little Country Church of Hollywood, 1934, Paul Kingsbury, 1750 North Argyle Avenue

Continue along on Argyle Avenue and you are back to where you started! You have now seen many of the architectural highlights of Hollywood!

Selected Bibliography

Gebhard, David, and Robert Winter. *Los Angeles: An Architectural Guide*. Layton, Utah: Gibbs Smith Publisher, 1994.

Gleye, Paul. *The Architecture of Los Angeles*. Los Angeles: Rosebud Books-The Knapp Press, 1981.

Herr, Jeffrey (ed.). *Landmark L.A.: Historic-Cultural Monuments of Los Angeles*. City of Los Angeles Cultural Affairs Department, Santa Monica, California: Angel City Press, 2002.

Kaplan, Sam Hall. *L.A. Lost and Found: An Architectural History of Los Angeles*. New York: Crown Publishers, 1987.

McGrew, Patrick and Robert Julian. *Landmarks of Los Angeles*. New York: Harry N. Abrams Publishers, 1994.

Index of Architects